WIRE WRAP JEWELRY

The Ultimate guide with simple tools and techniques for making awesome wire wrapped projects like earrings, pendants, beads and rings with ease

Katty Dennis

Table of contents

CHAPTER ONE

INTRODUCTION TO WIRE WRAPPING

Suggested Tools for Wire Wrapping

CHAPTER TWO

HOW TO MAKE A WIRE WRAPPED
CABOCHON PENDANT

CHAPTER THREE

HOW TO WIRE WRAP A BEAD

CHAPTER FOUR

HOW TO MAKE A WIRE WRAPPED
GEMSTONE RING

THE END

CHAPTER ONE

INTRODUCTION TO WIRE WRAPPING

Wire wrapping is grown to become a famous technique for jewelry making.it has open the ways to an entire exhibit of lovely jewelry designs without the requirement for loads of tools. These methods can fuse anything from gemstone beads or beads, gemstones cabochons to charms and simply unadulterated wire work. The accompanying pages give tips, guidance and procedures in various territories of wire wrapping and are open to all degrees of jewelry creators.

Suggested Tools for Wire Wrapping

Round nose pincers - for molding and bowing wire

Side cutters - for cutting wire

Kill nose pincers (otherwise called chain nose forceps) - incredible generally useful pincers, useful for molding and getting to hard to arrive at places

Level nose forceps - assists with making sharp corners in the wire

Then again, we additionally offer a total bunch of forceps and side cutters which incorporate the entirety of the above just as bent nose pincers (helpful for difficult to arrive at places) all these

comes in one handy case.

CHAPTER TWO

HOW TO MAKE A WIRE WRAPPED CABOCHON PENDANT

I have put together this instructional exercise on the best way to wire wrap a gemstone cabochon to make a lovely pendant. This venture utilizes one of our staggering spiderweb turquoise cabochons however you can utilize this method with any of your number one gemstones and decision of metal wire.

Follow carefully the step by step guide as listed here, and purchase all the gems making apparatuses and supplies you need online to get started.

Suggested Tools and Supplies

- Flat nose pincers

- Round nose forceps

- Wire cutters

- 3x 20cm of 0.6mm wire (authentic silver wire in this task)

- 2x 15-20 cm of 0.3mm wire (authentic silver wire in this task)

- Approx 18x13mm cabochon or another appropriate size (included: spiderweb turquoise cabochon)

- Tape measure/ruler

- Necklet chain

- Optional: clamp

FOLLOW MY STEP BY STEP TUTORIAL ON CREATING A WIRE WRAPPED PENDANT BELOW

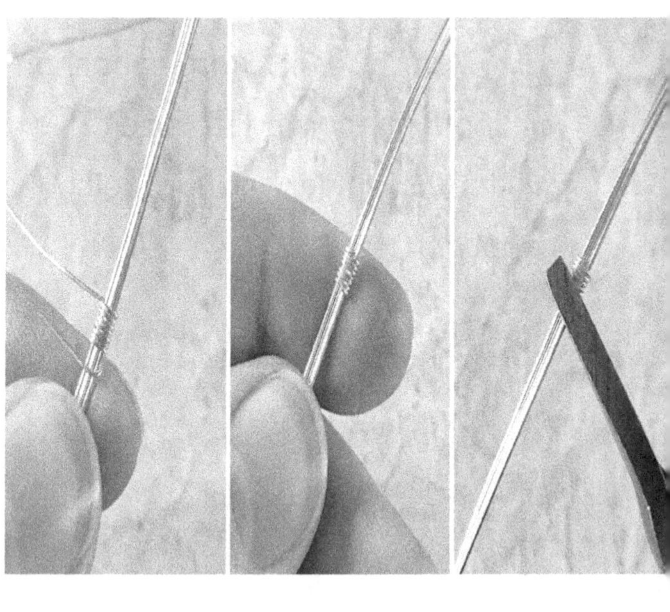

Take your 3 bits of 0.6mm 20cm base wires in a single hand, (in the event that you think that its simpler you can utilize a clamp to keep them straight), take 1 piece of the 0.3mm wire and in the wires, fold over the 3 base wires while holding them level around multiple times.

Cut the 0.3mm wire near the base wires with side cutters and utilize your level nose forceps to tenderly press together to make sure about.

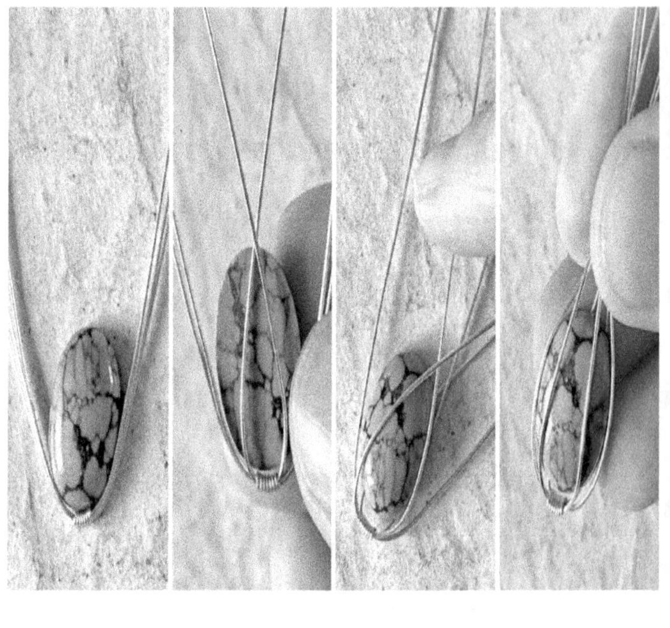

Position your cabochon down and with the joined wires at the base, tenderly curve the wires around the edges.

Turn your cabochon over in your grasp and tenderly draw the two back wires and get them over at the back, at that point turn the cabochon over and do likewise over the front of the stone.

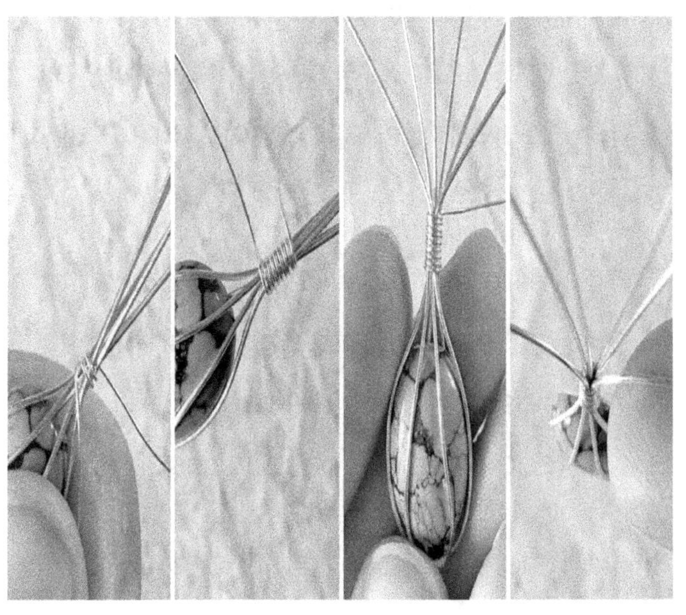

Bring all the wires around to the highest point of the cabochon and arrange.

Require your second piece of 0.3mm wire and wrap the wires together firmly, I did this around multiple times around, keeping the strain pleasant and educated to keep the cabochon set up and secure.

Trim off the wire with your side cutters and utilizing your level nose pincers, delicately press the end near the base wires.

Spread put your wires so two are looking ahead and two to one or the other side.

Delicately twist one wire aside and around the rear of the wrapped wires.

Fold over once ensuring the wire taught.

Utilizing your side cutters trim the wire, replicate this on the contrary side.

Whenever you have managed the two sides utilize your level nose forceps to make sure about the finishes against the base wires.

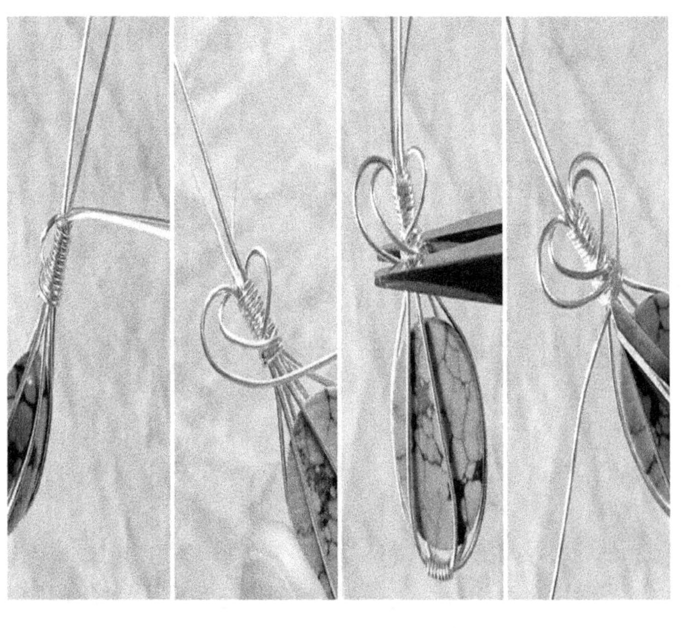

Go ahead and take the second wire along the edge of the 1st heart loop and fold over beneath the wires you have secured already.

Trim the wire with your side cutters and utilize level nose

pincers to tenderly press the wire to the base.

Replicate this process means on the opposite side.

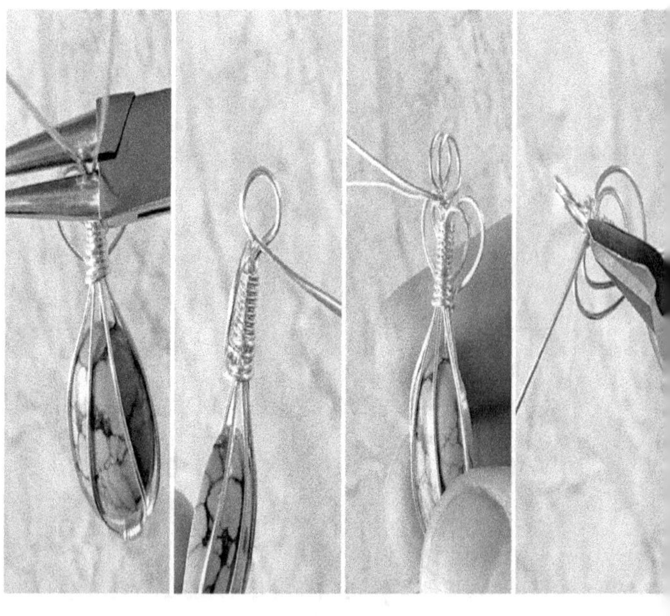

Take the last two wires and curve them advances to the front of the pendant.

Utilizing your round nose forceps, hold the wires as near the base as could reasonably be expected and twist them around the two wires on each side.

Take out the pincers and delicately twist around the front and to the back to ensure the loops are properly secured.

Your wire wrapped cabochon pendant is finished! Just add a string or chain to settle the piece prepared to wear.

CHAPTER THREE

HOW TO WIRE WRAP A BEAD

Wire wrapping a dot is a straightforward wire wrapping strategy however simply needs a little determination to create smart and steady outcomes.

When you have mastered the process, you will have the ability to make a wide scope of excellent gemstone jewelry.

The accompanying bit by bit guidelines tell the best way to make this method which is especially fit to utilizing with gemstone beads that have little openings. This is on the grounds that the 0.3mm (28 check) wire is extremely fine and adaptable and is extraordinary for wire wrapping.

Be that as it may, you can make similar impact with bigger holed beads and wires that are thick, it will simply be a smaller more troublesome! We suggest beginning little so you can dominate the procedure effortlessly.

- **Tools Needed**

- Side cutters

- Round nose forceps

- Snipe nose forceps

Components REQUIRED

- Metal wire - 0.3mm, check the wire will fit through your picked bead

- Gemstone bead

Adhere To Our Step By Step Instructions on How to Wire Wrap a Bead

Stage 1

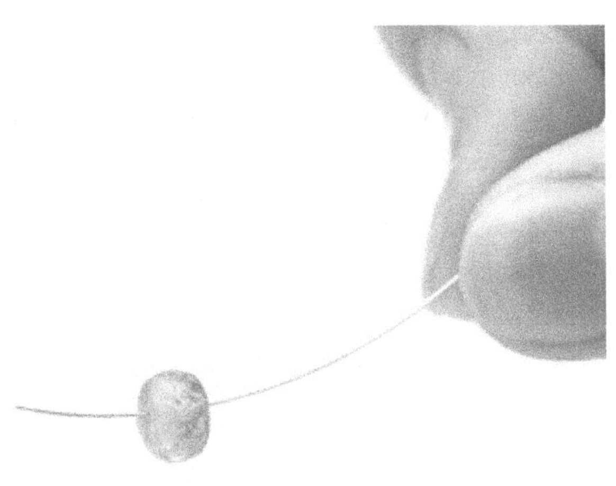

Cut a length of wire roughly 10cm long (it is simpler to have some additional wire than you will really use, as it gives you more to clutch while wrapping). Slip your dot onto the wire, leaving roughly

2cm toward one side (the
opposite end will be longer).

Stage 2

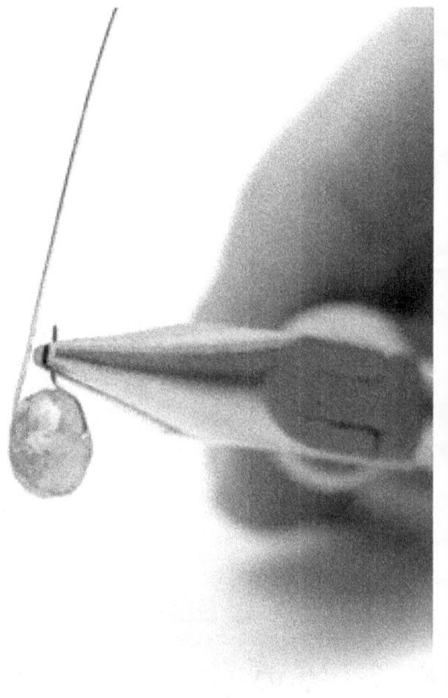

Squeeze or pinch the two finishes
of the wire together at the

highest point of the bead. Watch
that the bead is focused.

Stage 3

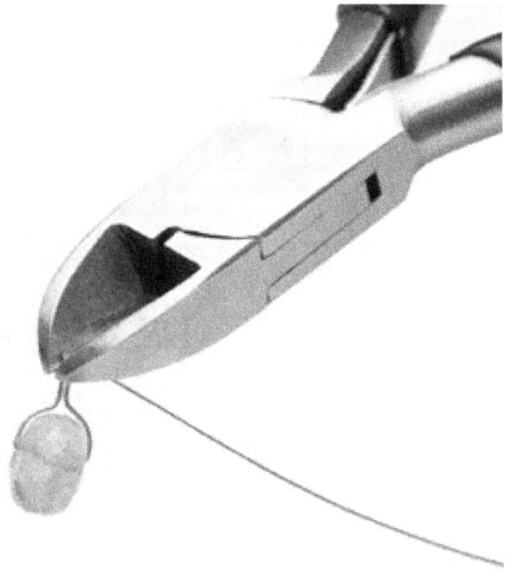

Remove the finish of the short
side of the wire utilizing side

cutters, so it is just around 2-3mm over the bead.

Stage 4

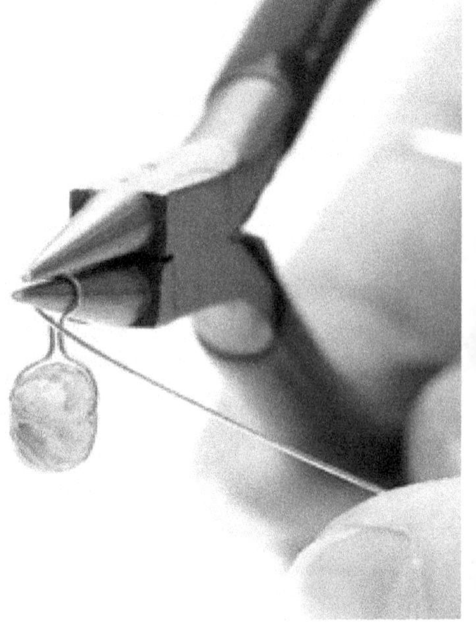

Next create a circle or loop with the more extended side of wire by bowing it to a correct point and folding it over the tip of your round nose pincers. Ensure the circle is over the finish of the short side of the wire and middle of the bead.

Stage 5

Utilizing kill nose forceps, hold the circle level between the tips. Take the long length of wire between your fingers and hold it taught. Begin folding it over the stem of the wires - beginning at the base of the circle and working down towards the bead. Ensure that each wrap sits perfectly and near the previous one.

Stage 6

At the point when you arrive at the highest point of the bead trim the end conveniently with side cutters. On the off chance that there is a sharp end left, twist it delicately with the kill nose pincers so it sits level and is tucked neatly away.

Wrapped up!

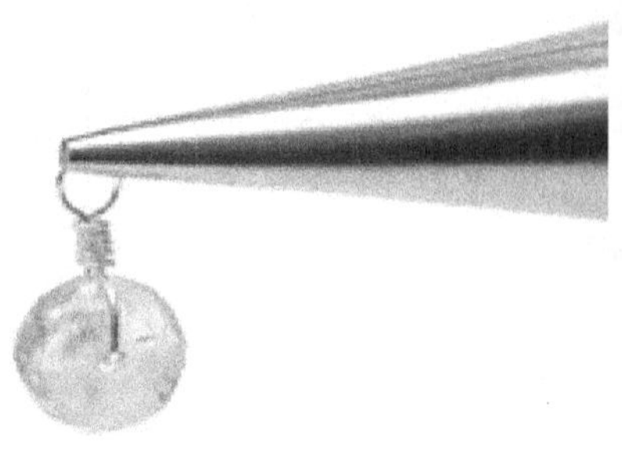

Your wrapped bead is presently completed and prepared to join into a wonderful adornments or jewelry design. Recall that this method takes practice (and a little persistence) to dominate. So continue on in the event that it doesn't look as you needed on your first endeavor or examination with the strategy until you discover a way that works for you.

Whenever you have dominated this strategy you will think that it's helpful for some, extraordinary beading projects. Wire wrapped beads like this can be joined with a hop ring to a part of chain and made into drop studs and pendants or connected to a wristband to make charms - the prospects are perpetual!

CHAPTER FOUR

HOW TO MAKE A WIRE WRAPPED GEMSTONE RING

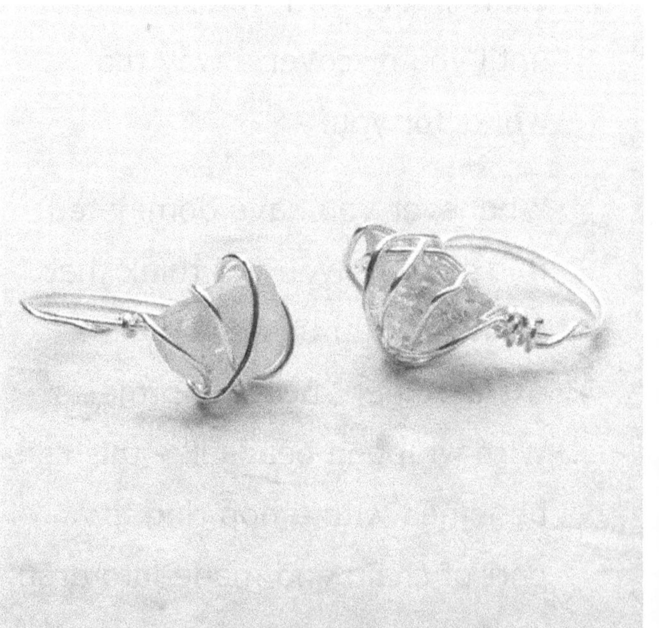

Wire wrapping is so well known and it's no big surprise with all the stunning and special designs you can make!

In this bit by bit instructional exercise, I tell you precisely the best way to make a wire wrapped ring utilizing a rough gemstone. Above we've utilized a similar procedure with a piece of ocean glass and harsh amethyst stone.

Wire-wrapping doesn't need any binding supplies, and with a couple of apparatuses required you can make a straightforward ring in a few minutes.

TIP: It's extraordinary to rehearse with plated silver wire as a spending alternative however know it's harder to work with than real silver which is considerably more malleable.

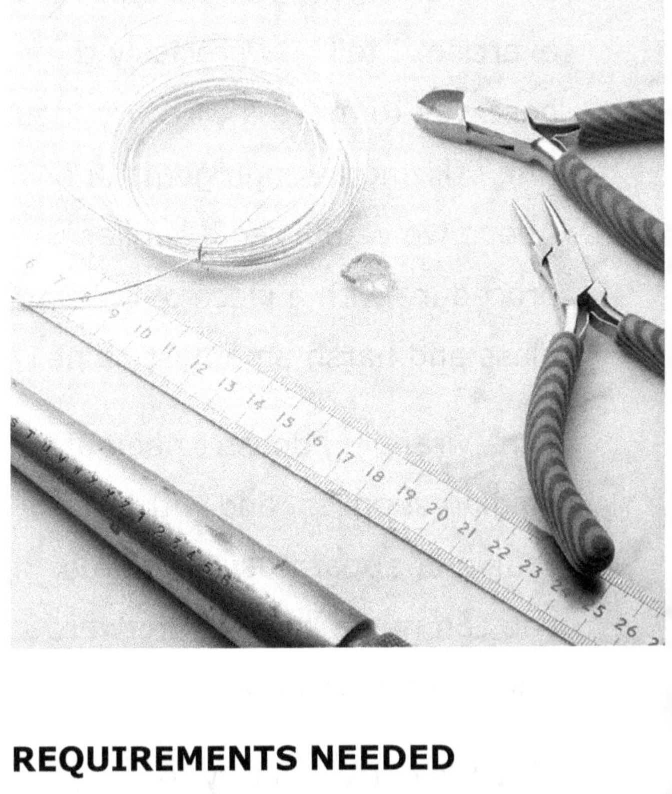

REQUIREMENTS NEEDED

40cm of 0.8mm authentic silver round wire

A rough gemstone you desire

Side cutters

Triblet

Level nose forceps

Snip nose forceps

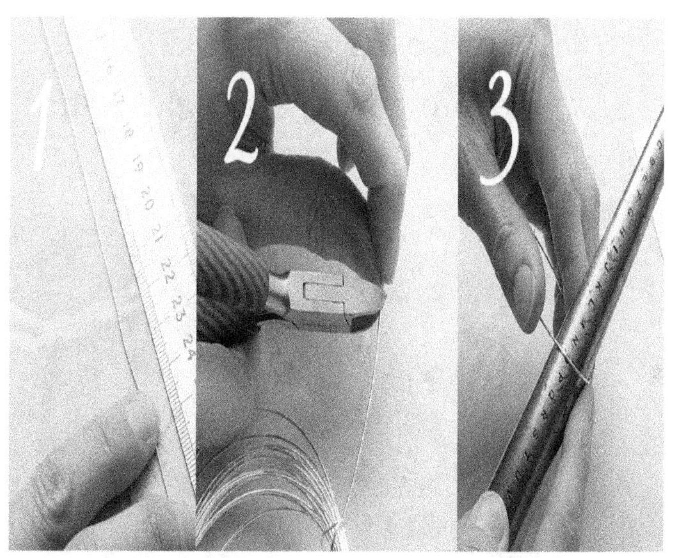

1. Lay the wire straight on a level surface and measure roughly 40cm.

2. Cut with side cutters - 40cm gives enough wire for your ring size and surplus wire for wrapping.

3. Start by tenderly twisting the wire into equal parts around the triblet.

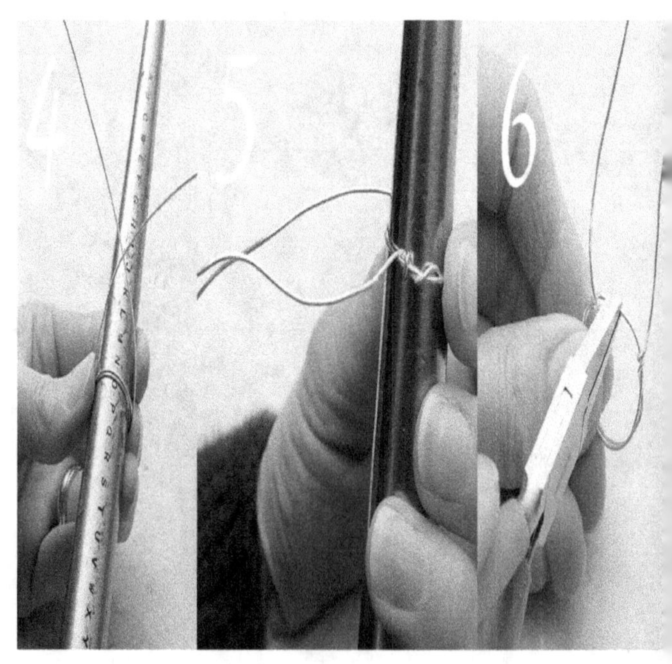

4. Place your wire work on the triblet on the position of the ring size that you'd preferred your ring to be. In the event that you don't have a ring triblet you can check out the house for something round to utilize, for example, a wooden spoon handle, pen or wooden dowels. Fold one finish of the wire over the triblet, leaving two loose ends.

5. With the two remaining loose ends at the front of the triblet, independently wrap each end under the wire ring a couple of wraps, leaving enough space for the length of your stone between them. These wraps on either side

will tie down the ring to a fixed size.

6. Position your level nose pincers where your stone will rest and utilize them to smooth the bend of the ring somewhat. This will give your stone a compliment surface to sit on, making it simpler to secure.

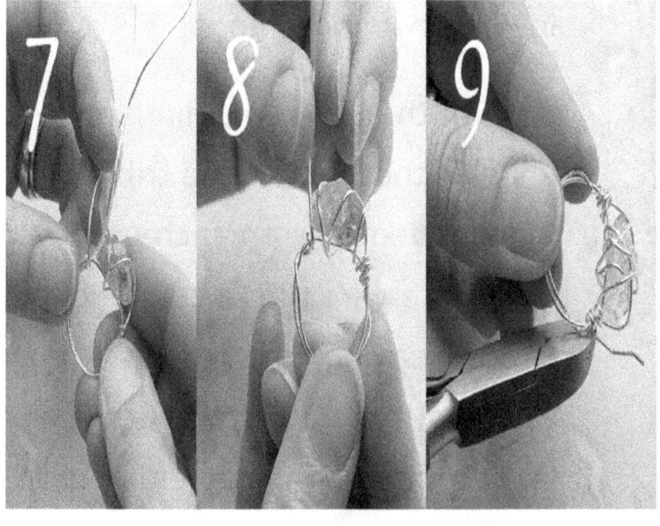

7. Hold the stone set up on the ring and fold one finish of the free wire over the stone to hold it set up. At the point when you run out of wire, fold additional circles over the side circles you made in sync 5 to make sure about set up.

8. Rehash stage 8 with the other piece of free wire and wrap at the contrary side, guaranteeing the stone is secure inside the wire wrap.

9. Utilize side cutters to clip off any free wire and use kill nose pincers to wrap up any loose ends that may exist. Position your ring

back on to the triblet and re-
shape to the right size.

Your ring is currently wrapped up!
Presently you know the method,
you can try by making more loops
and getting inventive with your
wire wrapping!

THE END